The Greenwoods SOLVE Proportions

Brandy Crump

Illustrations by RKS Illustrations

ISBN: 978-1-7335296-6-2

[ ] + − × ÷ = ? ( )

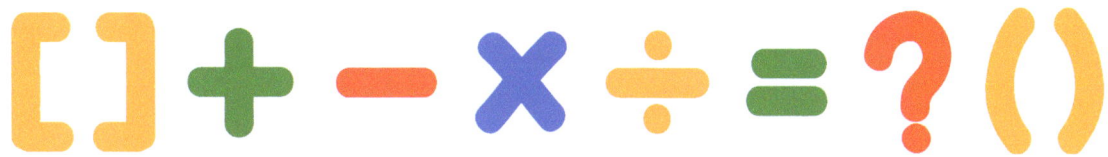

This book is dedicated to my baby that I miscarried in 2009. It was the pain of losing you that birthed this book series.

To my children, Myles and Bria, who inspire me to leave a legacy.

To Mr. Brown, former math teacher and coworker of 10 years, who kept asking me every single day, "Did you finish your books yet?" Well, Mr. Brown, I can finally say "YES!"

To Chris Nolen, former math teacher of 20 years and CEO of Nferno Productions, who read my manuscripts and said, "Hurry up and put those books out there!"

To the students who struggle in math and require simple explanations with examples of how it connects to their daily lives.

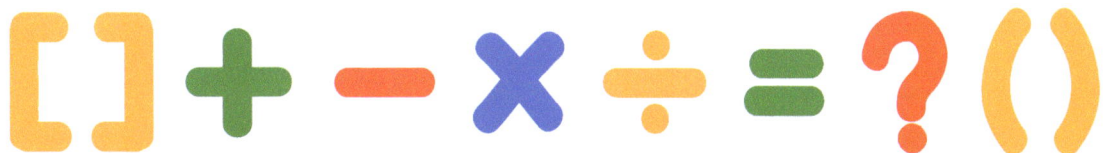

[ ] + − × ÷ = ? ( )

[ ] + − ✕ ÷ = ? ( )

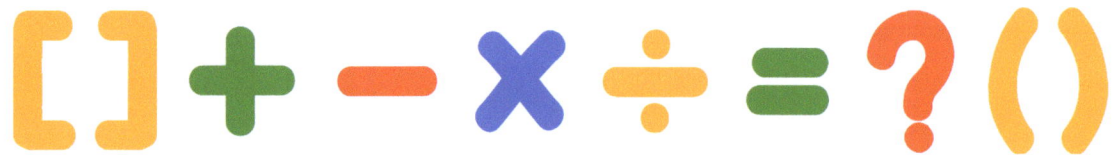

Miles woke up feeling under the weather. His nose was runny, throat was itchy, eyes were watery, and head was stuffy.

[ ] + − ✕ ÷ = ? ( )

[ ] + – ✕ ÷ = ? ( )

"Mom, I think my allergies are flaring up," said Miles. It's that time of the year again. The neighbors are cutting grass and the pollen is floating in the air daily.

[ ] + – ✕ ÷ = ? ( )

[ ] + − ✕ ÷ = ? ( )

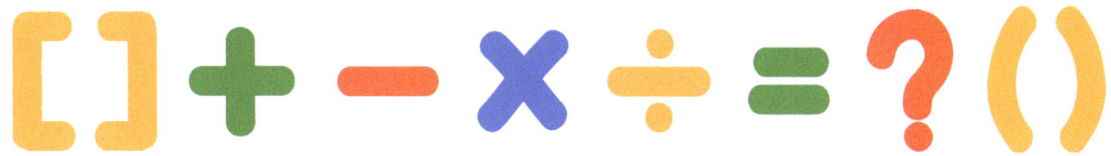

"You poor thing! Get the allergy medicine out of the medicine cabinet," said Mom. Miles immediately went into the bathroom, opened the medicine cabinet, and grabbed the one allergy medication that he found. Within a flash, Miles returned to Mom with the medication.

[ ] + − ✕ ÷ = ? ( )

[ ] + − × ÷ = ? ( )

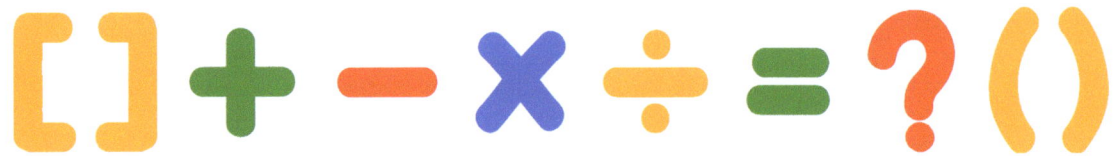

"Miles, this medicine is for children who weigh up to 95 pounds. Now that you weigh 125 pounds, you need the adult medication," said Mom. "Well, that's the only allergy medicine in there," said Miles.

[ ] + − × ÷ = ? ( )

[ ] + − ✕ ÷ = ? ( )

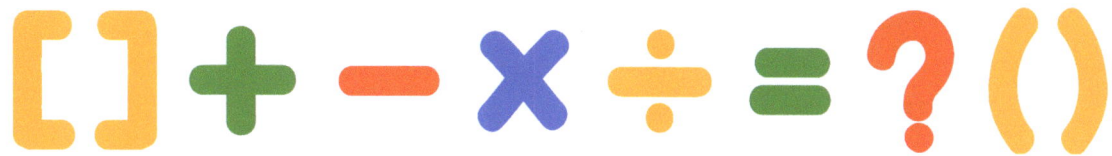

Mom looked at her watch and realized that it was only 7 am and the Harvey World Mart Store would not be open for another 2 hours; moreover, the closest 24-hour store was over an hour's drive away. Since going to the store to get some new medicine was not an option, Mom had to resort to plan B. Therefore, Mom decided to use the children's medication that she already had, which required her to convert the children's dosage to an adult dosage.

[ ] + − ✕ ÷ = ? ( )

[ ] + − × ÷ = ? ( )

Mom took the medication from Miles and read the label. It said the largest dosage was 10 ml for 95 pounds.

"Son, please give me a sheet of paper and a pencil so that we can calculate the dosage for your weight," said Mom.

[ ] + − × ÷ = ? ( )

[ ] + − ✕ ÷ = ? ( )

"Working as a nurse, I need to convert medication for my patients on a regular basis," she said. On the sheet of paper, Mom proceeded to write the following:

$$\frac{10 \text{ ml}}{95 \text{ pounds}} = \frac{x}{125 \text{ pounds}}$$

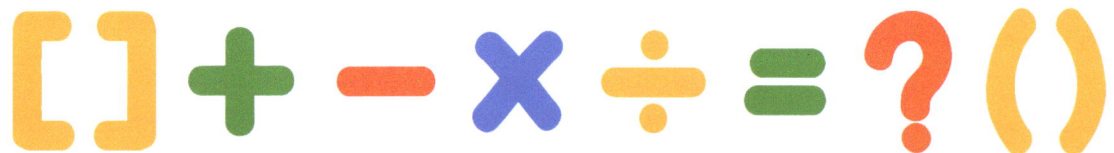

[ ] + − ✕ ÷ = ? ( )

[ ] + − × ÷ = ? ( )

Then Mom said, "We can set this problem up as a proportion, in other words, two equivalent ratios. We will write 10 ml over 95 pounds and set it equal to x (your unknown dosage) over 125 pounds (your weight).

[ ] + − × ÷ = ? ( )

Next, we will cross-multiply to solve the proportion by multiplying 10 times 125 and setting it equal to 95 times x to get

$$10 \times 125 = 95x$$
$$1250 = 95x$$

[]+ − ×÷ = ?()

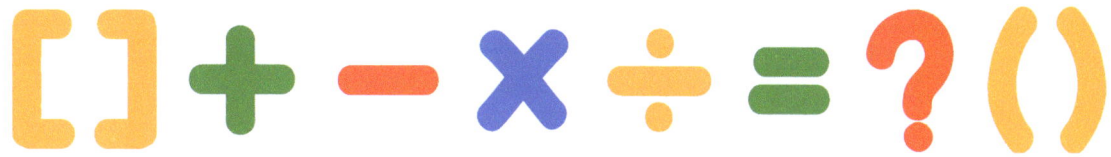

The last step is to solve for x by dividing both sides by 95. After dividing both sides by 95, the result is 13 ml." Miles took the allergy medication and then returned to bed to get some rest.

[]+ − ×÷ = ?()

[ ] + − × ÷ = ? ( )

Meanwhile, his little sister Brea and Mom were in the kitchen preparing macaroni and cheese for dinner. Mom usually cooks enough for 6 servings.

However, tonight the family is expecting around 50 guests to celebrate Grandma Greenwood's 65th birthday.

[ ] + − × ÷ = ? ( )

[ ] + − × ÷ = ? ( )

"Brea, my macaroni and cheese recipe requires 8 ounces of cheese for 6 servings. However, today we need 50 servings," said Mom.

"Well, how are we going to accomplish that, Mom?" Brea asked.

[ ] + − × ÷ = ? ( )

[ ] + − × ÷ = ? ( )

"We are going to use a proportion to solve this problem, Brea," Mom said.

Then Mom went to the drawer by the kitchen sink, pulled out a notepad, and wrote the following:

[ ] + − × ÷ = ? ( )

[ ] + − ✕ ÷ = ? ( )

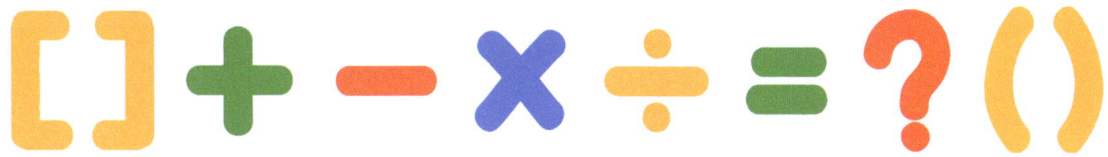

$$\frac{8 \text{ ounces}}{6 \text{ servings}} = \frac{x}{50 \text{ servings}}$$

"We must write 8 ounces over 6 servings and set it equal to x (the unknown ounces of cheese) over 50 servings," Mom said.

[ ] + − ✕ ÷ = ? ( )

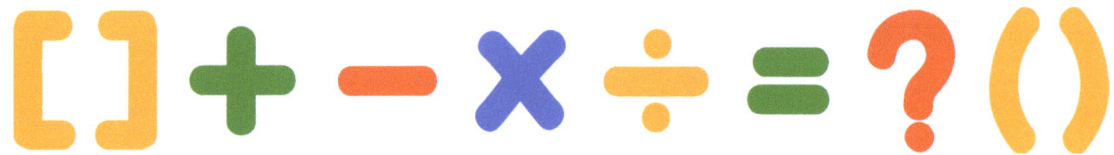

"The next step is to cross-multiply by multiplying 8 times 50 and setting that equal to 6 times x," said Mom. Then Mom wrote the following:

$$8 \times 50 = 6x$$
$$400 = 6x$$

[ ] + − x ÷ = ? ( )

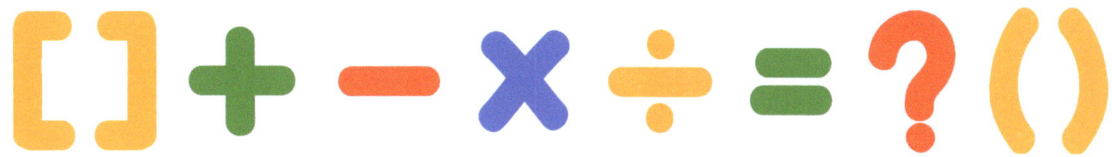

"Next, we must divide both sides of the equation by 6 because 6 is multiplied with x and to get rid of 6 you must do the opposite of multiplication, which is division," exclaimed Mom. Then Mom wrote the following:

[ ] + − x ÷ = ? ( )

[ ] + − × ÷ = ? ( )

$$\frac{400}{6} = \frac{6x}{6}$$

$$66.6 = x$$

"Thus, we need approximately 67 ounces of cheese for 50 servings of macaroni and cheese," Mom stated.

[ ] + − × ÷ = ? ( )

[ ] ✚ ━ ✖ ÷ = ? ( )

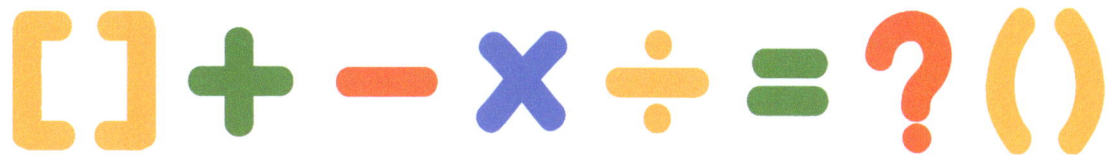

Mom and Brea went to the grocery store to purchase more cheese and then returned home quickly to cook dinner.

Later on, they observed with great pride as their family and friends ate and celebrated together.

[ ] ✚ ━ ✖ ÷ = ? ( )

[ ] + − × ÷ = ? ( )

Brandy Crump is the author of a math book series which includes the following titles: (1) The Greenwoods Add and Subtract Fractions with Like Denominators, (2) The Greenwoods Add and Subtract Fractions with Unlike Denominators, (3) The Greenwoods Multiply and Divide Fractions, (4) The Greenwoods Simplify Percents, (5) The Greenwoods Add and Subtract Integers, (6) The Greenwoods Solve One-Step Equations, and (7) The Greenwoods Solve Proportions. Brandy holds a bachelor's degree in Secondary Math Education and a master's degree in Educational Administration. She has 18 years of experience in teaching mathematics to at-risk students who suffer from adverse childhood experiences (ACES). She grew up in Harvey, Illinois, and graduated from Thornton Township High School where she taught for 14 years. As the product of an underserved, poverty-stricken, and high-crime community, she experienced ACES that prepared her to better understand and connect with her delinquent and at-risk students. She has provided workshops on effective classroom management through mutually respectful relationships and increasing student engagement through cooperative groups and authentic learning activities. Brandy is a lifelong learner and continues to research best practices for reaching out to struggling students. She is a member of Delta Sigma Theta Sorority Incorporated. She enjoys working with the youth in her community, writing books, creating math games, and conducting motivational speaking engagements.

[ ] + − × ÷ = ? ( )